Dalai Lama

Terry Barber

ACTIVIST
SERIES

Dalai Lama is published by
Grass Roots Press, a division of Literacy Services of Canada Ltd.

PHONE 1–888–303–3213
WEBSITE www.grassrootsbooks.net

ACKNOWLEDGMENTS

We acknowledge the financial support of the Government of Canada through the Book Publishing Industry Development Program (BPIDP) for our publishing activities.

We acknowledge the support of
the Alberta Foundation for the Arts
for our publishing programs.

Editor: Dr. Pat Campbell
Image research: Dr. Pat Campbell
Book design: Lara Minja, Lime Design Inc.

Library and Archives Canada Cataloguing in Publication

Barber, Terry, date
      Dalai Lama / Terry Barber.

ISBN 978-1-894593-90-8

      1. Bstan-dzin-rgya-mtsho, Dalai Lama XIV, 1935- 2. Dalai lamas—Biography. 3. Tibet (China) 4. Readers for new literates. I. Title.

PE1126.N43B3632 2008   428.6'2   C2008-901998-9

Printed in Canada

Contents

The Buddhist monks search for the boy.

The Search for the Dalai Lama

The men travel across Tibet. They search for the boy. The men must find the boy. They will not stop looking. The men feel they will find the boy soon. The men are **Buddhist monks**.

The Search for the Dalai Lama

A rainbow sits in the sky. The monks
follow the rainbow. It leads them to
a small hut. A little boy lives in the
hut with his family. Is this the boy the
monks are looking for?

The young boy.

The Search for the Dalai Lama

The family invites the monks into their home. It is a happy home. The monks can see that the parents love their children. The parents have five children. The youngest child is a boy. He is two years old.

The monk gives his beads to the boy.

The Search for the Dalai Lama

One of the monks wears a string of beads. The boy wants the beads. The monk tells the boy he can have them. First, the boy must answer a question. "Who am I?" the monk asks. The boy says, "You are a lama." The boy is right.

In Tibet, the word "lama" means "teacher."

The monks ask the boy to name objects.

The Search for the Dalai Lama

Buddhists believe people are reborn after death. The Buddhist monks test the boy's knowledge of his past life. The boy names objects he has never seen. He understands languages he has never heard. The boy passes the monks' tests with flying colours.

The
13th Dalai
Lama dies
in 1933.

The 13th Dalai Lama sits on his throne.

The Search for the Dalai Lama

The search is over. The monks have spent four years looking for the boy. They have found the 14th Dalai Lama. The boy is the **reincarnation** of the 13th Dalai Lama. One day, the boy will become Tibet's leader.

Dalai Lama means Ocean of Wisdom.

The Dalai Lama's parents and brothers.

Early Years

The boy is born on July 6, 1935. His parents name him Lhamo. His parents are poor farmers. They live a simple life in the high hills. Lhamo is different from his brothers and sisters. He is a serious child.

TIBET

●Lhasa

Early Years

It is 1937. The monks tell Llamo that he is the Dalai Lama. This news brings both joy and sorrow to his parents. Lhamo and his family must move to the city. The trip takes three months. Lhamo's parents miss their farm and friends.

The Dalai Lama and his family move to Lhasa in 1939.

Potala Palace in Lhasa, Tibet

Early Years

It is 1940. The Dalai Lama and his family move into a palace. He becomes the spiritual leader of Tibet. The Dalai Lama is only four years old. As the 14th Dalai Lama, he has much to learn.

The Dalai Lama and his family move into the Potala Palace.

The young Dalai Lama.

Early Years

The Dalai Lama begins his education.
He is just six years old. The lamas
teach the Dalai Lama. He learns math,
science, and history. He learns other
languages. The Dalai Lama learns fast
for such a young boy.

Buddha

Early Years

The Dalai Lama learns subjects far more important than math and science. He begins his Buddhist studies. He learns about the purpose of life. He learns about the meaning of life. One day, he will share this knowledge with the world.

The Tibetan flag.

Tibet

Tibet is an independent nation. The Tibetan people are free to practice their faith. They are free to speak their minds. Tibetans are free to go where they choose. They do not go hungry. They lead good lives.

Tibet is called the Rooftop of the World.

Kyrgyzstan

Mongolia

China

TIBET

● Lhasa

Nepal

Bhutan

India

Bay of Bengal

Tibet

Tibet is in the centre of Asia. It sits between India and China. India and China are Asia's most powerful countries. In 1949, China **invades** Tibet. China wants Tibet to become part of China. The people of Tibet want the Dalai Lama to be their political leader.

Over 80,000 Chinese troops invade Tibet on October 7, 1950.

The Dalai Lama sits on his throne in 1950.

Tibet's Leader

The Dalai Lama is 15 years old. He has been Tibet's spiritual leader for ten years. Now, he must take charge of Tibet. In 1950, the Dalai Lama becomes Tibet's head of state. He is both the spiritual and political leader of Tibet.

The Dalai Lama is the leader of 6 million people.

The Dalai Lama meets with the Chinese leaders.

Tibet's Leader

In 1951, the Chinese force Tibet to sign a **treaty**. The Chinese take control of Tibet. The people of Tibet suffer under Chinese rule. In 1954, the Dalai Lama meets with Chinese leaders. He tries to make peace.

The Chinese **repress** Tibet's identity, culture, and language.

Tibetan monks surrender to the Chinese.

Escape into Exile

In 1959, Tibet **rebels** against Chinese rule. Tibet does not succeed. The Dalai Lama flees to India. He is not afraid of death. But he knows he must stay alive to keep hope alive. The Tibetan people need him to stay alive.

The Dalai Lama escapes to India with 80,000 Tibetans.

Escape into Exile

Since 1959, China has been hard on Tibet. Over 1.2 million Tibetans have died. Many other Tibetans are in prison. They are put in prison for being Buddhist. They are put in prison for wanting a free Tibet.

The Tibetans are victims of hunger, torture, and killings.

The Dalai Lama holds the Nobel Peace Prize.

Escape into Exile

The Dalai Lama still lives in **exile**.
He lives in India, but his heart lies in
Tibet. He wants China to give Tibet
more freedom. The Dalai Lama's
weapons are truth, justice, and
courage. He does not want to gain
freedom through violence.

The Dalai Lama gets the Nobel Peace Prize in 1989.

The Dalai Lama speaks to a crowd of people.

The Dalai Lama's Message

Today, the Dalai Lama is known around the world. He gives speeches in different countries. More people than Buddhists listen to his message. People from all walks of life listen to his message. He is one of the world's great leaders.

The Dalai Lama has spoken to people in 65 countries.

The Dalai Lama prays for peace.

The Dalai Lama's Message

The Dalai Lama talks about building a better world. He promotes human values such as peace. He talks about the importance of world peace. He promotes religious harmony. He wants the different religions to respect one another.

The Dalai Lama promotes compassion, wisdom, self-discipline, tolerance, and forgiveness.

The Dalai Lama's Message

The people of Tibet love their country and culture. The Dalai Lama speaks for Tibetans. The Dalai Lama spreads his message about Tibet's struggle for freedom. The world listens. The world waits and hopes for Tibet's freedom.

A Tibetan man prays for freedom.

Glossary

Buddhist: a person whose religion is Buddhism.

exile: to force someone to live in another country.

invade: to enter by force to conquer.

monk: a male member of a religious community. He lives under vows of poverty, chastity, and obedience.

rebel: to fight against one's ruler.

reincarnation: rebirth of the soul in a new body.

repress: to restrict the freedom.

treaty: an agreement between two nations.

Talking About the Book

What did you learn about the Dalai Lama?

What did you learn about Tibet?

Do you think Tibet will regain its freedom?

What does freedom mean to you?

The Dalai Lama learns about the purpose of life. In your opinion, what is the purpose of life?

Picture Credits